A Ship Called Destiny
Yvonne's Book

BOOKS BY PETER TROWER

POETRY

Poems for a Dark Sunday (mimeo)
Moving Through the Mystery
Between the Sky and the Splinters
The Alders and Others
Ragged Horizons
Bush Poems
Goosequill Snags
The Slidingback Hills
Unmarked Doorways
Where Roads Lead
Hitting the Bricks
Chainsaws in the Cathedral
A Ship Called Destiny: Yvonne's Book
There are Many Ways (forthcoming)

PROSE

Rough and Ready Times (with Ellen Frith)
Grogan's Cafe (novel)
Dead Man's Ticket (novel)
The Judas Hills (novel)

WEBSITE — http://www.hushdata.com/ptrower/

A Ship Called Destiny

Yvonne's Book

Poems of Travel and Love

Peter Trower

Ekstasis  Editions

Canadian Cataloguing in Publication Data

Trower, Peter
    A ship called Destiny: Yvonne's book.

    Poems
    ISBN 1-896860-77-X

       I. Title.
    Ps8555.H668C38   2000   C811'.54   C00-910489-5
    PR9199.3.C497C38   2000

Acknowledgements:

Some these poems originally appeared in *Moving Through the Mystery*,
Goosequill Snags; *The Slidingback Hills*; *Unmarked Doorways*; *Where
Roads Leads*, *Hitting the Bricks*; *Sunshine Coast News* and *B.C. Studies*.
The remainder have never seen print before.

Published in 2000 by:
Ekstasis Editions Canada Ltd.   Ekstasis Editions
Box 8474, Main Postal Outlet   Box 571
Victoria, B.C. V8W 3S1   Banff, Alberta ToL oCo

THE CANADA COUNCIL | LE CONSEIL DES ARTS
FOR THE ARTS | DU CANADA
SINCE 1957 | DEPUIS 1957

A Ship Called Destiny: Yvonne's Book has been published with the assistance of
a grant from the Canada Council and the Cultural Services Branch of British
Columbia.

CONTENTS

Author's Introduction

This book is a tribute to my long-time partner, best friend and soulmate, Yvonne Klan. Many of the poems involve journeys both physical and emotional, that I would undoubtedly never have taken without her unstinting encouragement, inspiration and love. She has been my muse in a very real sense.

In the fall of 1982, we undertook what would prove to be our most far-ranging odyssey. The underlying motive for the trip was to track down information on a devious ex-preacher known as The King of the Safecrackers — and we did this — but it turned out to be much more than that. It produced a series of poems unlike any I had ever written before. These poems, starting with *Big Bang Still Echoing* and ending with *We Measure the Mile in Muffets*, are presented here in full and proper sequence for the first time. While we took numerous other trips that also triggered decent poems, this was a definite high point.

So, as the title implies, this is very much Yvonne's Book. She has been my invaluable companion on so many adventures. I owe her more than I can ever say or repay.

Peter Trower
January 10, 2000

THE SHIP
for Yvonne

Forty years after the fact
we stand by a long-closed schoolhouse
in the same smoke-haunted pulpmilltown
where we first met at fourteen
Darkly seductive even then
you vamped me on a bet
"Hello, big boy," you purred
My face burned red   I died with shyness

But in time's sensible turning
the shyness melted to love
Now we walk hand in hand
across an old swinging bridge

Down by the sea where the dock once stood
an ancient ship hangs at anchor
derelict whaler livid with rust
as we watch it turns in the wind
The prow comes into view
we gasp in disbelief
an aura of strangeness transfigures the day
the name of the ship is Destiny.

TRAIL
for Yvonne

Walking hand in hand
down that obscure trail
in whispering spring
we celebrate
our old youth   our new love
in the protected splendour
of this much-wended forest

Around us:
gnarled headless cedars —
moss-cloaked stumps of longago defilements —
squirrelled, bird-thronged undergrowth —
still air, chill with fading winter —
woodland pools, some brown and dismal
clogged with last year's leaves —
others greenly exultant with new plant life

Above us:
branch-latticed sky

Beneath our feet:
packed, reassuring earth

In a small clearing
a Native canoe maker
wise with many years
looks up from his chiselling
smiles understandingly
approvingly at us as we pass

And although
the rain-pulped cigarette packages —
the bleaching gum wrappers
belie this place to be other than what it is
it seems for a spellbound moment
a pristine Arcady
as we embrace
lost in the utter wonder
of each other.

A WILD GIRL TO WALK THE WEATHERS WITH
for Yvonne

On bleak or blistering days
mountain-goating the hard tilting hills
in gaunt ice-carved valleys
slide-scarred
headstoned with the high-notched stumps
of earlier invasions,
I fear no more the dancing deadly rigging
the sudden sidewinding logs
the down-thundering boulders
for life has opened
and I have at last
a wild girl to walk the weathers with

In other camps   valleys   years
I moved in terror
between the lashing lines
and the not-loving
the not-being-loved
burned more deeply than the fear

But though the hazards remain
ubiquitous as ever
they are endurable now
for life has opened
and I have at last
a wild girl to walk the weathers with

GOSPEL ROCK AWAKENING

After the muttonfat winter
spring comes suddenly and late
like the point of a joke
to a sluggish mind

Sprung
from the prison of myself
I walk through new born brilliance
the warm   winding
arbutus-sentried road

Below the religious rock
inscribed laboriously
by some long ago zealot,
the sun has pried open
the small glittering eyes of the sea
They blink out before me
like startled flecks of gold
towards a horizon of mist

Here it was
we once, clinging tightly,
kissed in the hazel drift
of another year
It was raining   or had rained
A different jury of clouds
gazed dispassionately down —
found us guilty of love

Your lips whisper to me still
from beyond the time screen
I feel your soft warmth against me
in this warm-memoried place

You have drifted away
into another man's april
but the ghost of your sweetness
will linger always
in these spring-struck vistas

Old Love; New Summer

We had swum in one warm and evening sea
and now,
sharing illicit cigarettes
on the fallen log above the steep path,
we prepared to swim in another

They were quick in coming
the subtle waves,
lifting us
to that plane of dazzling sorcery
one remove from reality
or perhaps
one step further into it

In a clearing
surrounded by rustlings and magic
we clung together
and later lay
fantasizing the Sistine Chapel dome
of leaf-frescoed sky
into oceans   animals   faces —
michelangeloes
of a special twilight

In this closed private universe
we floated
one mind at last —
higher than the hill
or height

Until,
undone by watch edicts,
we descended
from fond, found Eden
the near-vertical trail
to the other summer.

THE BEGINNING AGAIN

Ironic cackle of a duck
derisive in the dawn
waves like whispering explosions
along the shore
boats stuttering alive
hungry to hit the fishward trail
time beginning again
for them   for us

Greek chorus of awakening
cats piteous at the door
one single distant dog bark
your soft still half-dreaming voice
incredibly discreet creak
of the mattress as we embrace
time clicking the switches back on
for us   for them

This secret scenario
was thus since God first cast the dice
it is the miracle of recommencing
after our little deaths in the darkness
it is mortality's song
orchestrated before sunrise
it is the simple hymn of rebeing
the beginning again.

RIM SONG

White man's time ceases
watches break down
on beaches luminous with autumn
the wind owns
All things shatter into seeing
truth speaks
on beaches broader than believing
where lies break

Through gnarled and gale-twisted snags
tanglewoods of stormed alders
man-dwarfing jungles of salal
we have attained the world's shoulder
You have led me to this high knoll
where we can see in all directions
brought me through darkness to the light
We have transcended mere affection

Briefly you slip away from me
to walk those infinite perspectives
I sit transfigured by our love
a glad and dedicated votive
The mauling rollers curl and crash
birds flee inflooding water
chitter to the security of rocks
I am the watcher and the waiter

Then you ineffably return
and render all the glories lesser
Your smile is warmer than the sun
I am the winner, not the loser
Words cannot encompass these emotions
I clutch you to me like a clown
White man's time ceases
and all the watches break down.

Escape From the Jewel Box

A lone jet shivering light
falls in across the dusk-blurred sky
behind the jewel-box city
that reaches ruby-tipped towers
like sceptres of black and gold
into the slow sweep of twilight
Night is climbing to us
down the ladders of the evening

Through the city's gem-strung mazes
my old selves wander yet
seeking truth   lies   oblivion
stumbling under life
through chimera kingdoms
where streetlights blink false signals
The jewels in that box conceal poison
like stones in a Borgia ring

Night is climbing to us
down the ladders of the evening
and I have escaped the treacherous jewel box
Lady of impossible hopes
you lie silken beside me
a treasure more precious than gems
You have transmuted my fool's-gold life
with the warm alchemy of your love.

AMONG THE DEADHEADS
for Yvonne

Like the broken bones
of huge long-extinct creatures
the salvaged deadheads lie in bleaching heaps
among the carapaces   the rust-reddened corpses
of old machinery
above the beach stones   the eel grass
to rest again
on the land that once lifted them tall
in this bay of twin creeks   remote memories

Thirty years of booming have beaten this place
into a shabby echo
of what existed before —
the gyppo sawmill beside the lost estate
of my Norwegian aunt   her hospitable house
filled with the smells of baking —
singsong accents and laughter

Yesterday phantoms this bludgeoned cove
like an exposed photograph —
what was still flickers dimly against the alders —
the fool boy I left here   the vibrant girl you were
run yet through an ache of time
from the creepy throat of a rock-cricket cave —
play hearts by the sputtering light
of a naptha lamp —
gasp as a seal breaks sudden water
by our rowboat's bow like a drowned-man's head

Sad in the utterness of change
we search in vain for random traces
of that other reality   those simpler selves
But where my aunt's house stood is only a cat-road —
the rowboat's a fish palace under the log booms —
even the sawmill's pilings are gone
and the dreams of our youth lie scattered forlornly
among the bone-white deadheads.

REMNANTS

Among those melancholy hills
the dead farm lives
ragged curtains
loll like grey tongues
from silent windows

Relic of the high hollows
where they once read Liberty
in nineteen thirty-eight
western pulp magazines
yellowing in a shed
ancient religious tracts
long-shredded by rats

Stubborn they must have been
those vanished pioneers
settling to a scrub ledge
in a hardscrabble land
The sadness of their thwarted venture
is told in weather-scuffed wood
sagging monuments of their labour
incline to the soil
antique automobiles rust
beyond the dry well
a half-buried ploughshare
lies where they left it

Inside, forgotten clothes
hang where they hooked them
grimy bib overalls
a frayed greatcoat
Upstairs, mouse droppings
his going-to-meeting tie
torn mattresses
crumpled letters full of bad news

They are forty years gone from their failure
in these bleak upland meadows
now we must follow their memories west
brushing the ghosts from our shoulders.

THE GUESTS

Around our wilderness mountaintop table
the guest begin to gather
an incursion of the small
chittering twittering closer
circling through the sun-circled afternoon

Like fencers they advance and retreat
wary eyes take our measure
prudently they hesitate
but the lure of the crumbs proves too strong
their forest caution deserts them

Quick squirrels dart to the booty
whiskeyjacks filch from our fingers
a tiny stouthearted chipmunk
scales the ramp of my hand
with thistledown feet and attains the prize

It is a scene out of Francis of Assissi
a nature film by Walt Disney
the small have offered their trust
and we are the guests   not they
scattering our tithes in a highcountry clearing.

THE ABANDONED ALEXANDRA BRIDGE

Rendered obsolete
by cleverer technology
the castaway span still stands
joining two fragments of disused road
once a sterling accomplishment
now a rusting anachronism
like something after a nuclear war
when civilization has crumbled

Graduation Day graffiti
disfigures the approaches
like all the rainbow rocks and cliffs
they've sullied with spray cans
but the bridge stands stolidly
leading from nowhere to nowhere
spanning an historic river
become history in turn

Across that torrent now
is only a native fish trap
the shore reverts to primal purposes
You pick wild strawberries
by a wild orchard of unpruned cherry trees
I kiss your strawberry lips
and hold you close
at the dead span's centre
while the muddy flood churns beneath us
and Simon Fraser's ghost
laughs silently from the cliffs.

HELL'S GATE

At Hell's Gate that great
wallow of water
a million gallons of ramming thrust
squeezes through the canyon's narrowest throat
in a tumbling thunder
of foam and elemental fury

Once history
ran rampant as the river between these cliffs
headless armless miners
swam its grim flood in the goldrush massacres
and the gallant paddleboat Scuzzy
battled its way uptorrent
against all odds and the current
in 1881

An even century later
I swallow my acrophobia
and ride that spidery tramcar with you
over and down to the gorge's bottom
Here where explorers once gnawed on pemmican
we breakfast on bacon and eggs
The hounds of hell have been brought to heel
and the legends reduced to expensive books
in the souvenir shop.

Painted Chasm

Great ragged red gouge
in the hard flesh of the ground
trees tightrope-walking
the crumbling brink
brush-bottomed dry gulch —
carving river long vanished
poor man's Grand Canyon
lost in Caribou Country

We stand close together
at the dizzy echoing edge
tossing random pebbles
that spin down forever
"My mother once told me
this is where a Scotsman
dropped a nickel," you laugh
putting it all into perspective.

No Breeze On Lake Louise

No breeze on Lake Louise
only ice locking it silent
between those overexposed mountains
So much of this place
has been borne away on film
it seems obscurely diminished

Group tours tumble from buses
by that incongruous hotel
multi-roomed and pretentious
looming behind us
like some misplaced palace —
the last gasp of empire

Ghost strains of that simple-minded song
guylombardo through the drizzle
Grizzled last romantics
stroll hand in hand through honeymoon memories
and you and I, my darling, stroll with them
needing no breeze to fan our new love.

THE PEAKS
for Yvonne

Impossible Rockies
explode around us
wind-fretted escarpments
buckle up into blue
cloud-flagged   primordial
bare bent teeth of the world
snow spittled gnaw the blank sky

Each twist of the highway
pits us against fresh vistas
trees storm up from manless valleys
to thin and fail against granite
the peaks   the peaks   the peaks
god thrones and goblin castles
grotesque formations crowning a crag-top
like ruins on a dead planet

Only a fool or a blind man
could fail to gasp in their presence
the mute fact of their vastness
the majesty of their shambling march
they mammoth up   crescendoes of stone
a spectacle beggaring words
as two small ant things scuttle by
drunk on the pure wine of wonder

TAY JOHN COUNTRY

Rattling down the Yellowhead
from Jasper in the gloom
of a sunless day
past dull slate-grey lakes
glowering cliffs where clouds and shadows
cling like cobwebs
towns that don't exist
and monstrous Mount Robson
looming through the mist

Rattling down the Yellowhead
across the timid birth trickle
of the Fraser River
bound to burgeon and build
into a rampaging flood —
a muddy Amazon of power
before it marries the distant sea

Rattling down the Yellowhead
where Tay John cut his legend
like a packtrail
through the underbrush of history
made his famous cache
for no man's knowledge but his own
in the heyday of the fur brigades

Rattling down the Yellowhead
through past and present
out of darkness into sunlight
and dusty Valemount
raw railside town
to make our twilight bivouac
at another anonymous motel

RECESSION IN FRASER'S VALLEY

Prodigious river
sprung from that meagre stream
we wondered on in the Yellowhead country
welling enormous now
through widening floodplains

Windbrooms slapping up
sandstorms from the sandbars
like dust from dirty rugs

Trumpeter swans
trading mournful choruses
in reedy sloughs

Bypassed whistlestop towns
full of boarded-up stores
dreaming of likelier days

Indifferent freight trains
bound for anywhere but there
barrelling nonstop through

Abandoned silo leaning drunkenly
rotting Tower of Pisa
glum against the sky

Lastgasp resorts
offering rundown cabins
for tourists who never come

Ramshackle bus shelters
tattooed with obscenities
and sinister swastikas

Three wise eagles
minding their own business on a branch
beside a brackish backwater

Hear no eagle
See no eagle
Speak no eagle

GRINDROD

Just a blink of a town
a clutch of farms
a crackerbarrel store
drowsing by a listless river
not a bad place to grow up in perhaps
but hardly a high point
on anyone's journey
yet the odd name sticks in my mind

Back in the Alcazar bar
days later
I nurse an inflationary beer
as the minutes to bus-time trick by

A redneck insults a black
a nodding-out junkie gets bounced
a small loquacious shabby man
sits down at the next table

"Just got in from Medicine Hat," he announces
"I'm a farmer   carpenter   sawmill hand
Lookin' to find my brother
Lives in some little burg called Grindrod"

Two weeks before
the name would have rung no bells at all
Now I even have a Government map
Like a tourist guide, I show him the way

He leaves with a terse thanks
to search for unknown people
in a town I have only glimpsed fleetingly
I imagine him shambling drunkenly
unexpectedly   likely unwanted
into obscure Grinrod
expounding windily
in the crackerbarrel store
increasing the population by one
beside that listless river.

Harrison Hot Springs Nocturne

Snow wind whistles
from high muffled peaks
tourist town crouches
on the rim of dark waters
achingly remote
lighthouse blinks wanly
steam wreathes the sulphur springs
like ghosts of fur traders

Laughter within
old friends   new meetings
amberlit ambience
of the lakeside hotel
plunging and lazing
in the earth-heated water
safe as unborn things
in the amniotic pool

Without, the winter
prowls like a stalker
through abandoned houses
along wide empty streets
totem poles shiver
in the long wind of history
lonely in his hill cave
the last sasquatch sleeps.

UNDER ANOTHER VOLCANO

In the uncertain setting
of a church become a tavern
we sit on a sacrilegious Sunday
talking of poems and murder

Scarcely an hour before
we were drinking wine in the winy air
of the high country
staggered by alpine enormities
valleys scooping vastly   down and away
through indigo distances —
scarps of ancient lava
crumbling vomit of old eruptions —
naked cragwalls across the north sky
where no tree clings nor ever will —
cloud-shrouded bulk
of inscrutable Mount Baker
mysterious as God
nursing its dormant fires

Now we have descended
from the sublime to the bizarre —
they have pews for chairs in this place —
the bar is where the pulpit stood —
the cans are in the sacristy —
the crowd looks obscurely sinister —
I swear I hear a guy
order a bourbon and holy water

Now I'm no bible-thumper
but I don't believe in tempting Providence either
After all, who knows?
This place makes me nervous
As we leave I notice
they don't even have a lightning-rod
These jokers
are really asking for trouble.

On The Pitt Lake Dike

Sunlight pulling up stakes
in late afternoon —
peeling back from the peaks —
letting shadows slat down
into the scree-shattered valleys
of old Slumach's broken land
where once he stalked wild as the cliff goats —
found the mine no man would strike again —
toted out the gold that fired a legend —
drank himself deranged in New Westminster —
took a white whore for his woman —
slew the man who sought his secret —
died with it on the Queen's gallows
leaving just his angry ghost to prowl
those devil's-clubbed wastes   luring
greedy unwary searchers to disaster

On the Pitt Lake dike
only our minds evoke the old violences —
the ebbing day is narcotic with peace
We stroll the deserted levee idly
thoughts slipping from Slumach
imagining now stolid gangs of Dutchmen
rearing this arduous wall in the flood years —
thrusting the waters back
with the same lowcountry stubbornness
that stayed the North Sea —
transforming bog to polder   marsh to meadow
grafting a piece of Holland
richer   more enduring than lost gold mines
on this drowned land that no man wanted

Sunlight pulling up stakes
in late afternoon
We start the long carward walk
talking of angry Slumach   bland tenacious Dutchmen —
the strange anomalies of human need.

BIG BANG STILL ECHOING

When that dyspeptic volcano
finally blew its top
this unlucky piece of country
had a reluctant preview
of World War Three
but it was Nature who pushed the button
not the Russians

They say
the sky was black with dust that day
a scalding colossal flatulence
broke from the bowels of the earth
and mud flowed like water
down the Toutle River

Whole forests
fell over like jackstraws
and stubborn hermit Harry Truman
went to join his famous namesake
hammered into oblivion
along with the lake he loved

Now, two years later, the land
still reels from the memory
Uncleared ash heaps bear witness
to that apocalyptic moment

Beside the Toutle River
twelve feet of hard-packed silt
furnish a buried house
Opportunistic vendors
try to profit from disaster
with t-shirts   posters   ash-sculptures
Brash gaudy billboards
proudly proclaim this to be
the *Volcano Capital of America*

And the mountain
called St. Helen's
hides primly
behind a cloud blanket
never to be taken for granted
again.

A Brown Town in Oregon

Sunk in the freeway's backeddy
two miles east under mountain shadow
a town named Brownsville
that must have been somewhere once
glooms beside a somnolent river
that jumps its banks more springs than not
by the look of punchdrunk houses on sodden foundations
sagging false-front stores on false-hope streets
the stained ancient drugstore on a corner
where bored kids loiter
This is a place of fitful functionings
they are past depression doom-talk here —
this place has been depressed for decades

Thus the paradoxical incongruity
of a modern well-appointed library
neat as a new nickel
set like a bright island
in a sea of shabbiness   ruin and apathy

Here, not far from the derelict Baptist church
where Holy Herb Wilson once preached,
the heart of the town resides
In a small room of local history
painstaking records
touch the lost pulse of the past —
enshrine what was in a special place

But only yesterday lives in this town
Today is like the gnarled   dying
grotesquely-twisted tree
in the dank weed-choked yard we pass as we leave
Tomorrow does not compute.

SHADOW OF SAN QUENTIN

All dusty day
we drum through Steinbeckian landscapes
of a stultifying sameness

to reach a great blowing bay
with causewayed tideflats
San Francisco across the water

Brief glimpse
of that old fortress of sorrows
glooming on a headland

Incongruous mission name —
they called it *The Old Spanish Prison*
in the days before the earthquake

Monument to sordid deeds
and aborted hopes
laying its cold touch on the countryside

The King of the Safecrackers
spent twelve long years here —
we think of him dully

Tacky motel
in uneasy San Rafael
in the shadow of San Quentin

Fitful sleep in fusty heat
Sudden noise jarring us awake
Something at the window!

Visions of escaped convicts
insidious invasion
homicidal lunatics with knives

Only a gaunt stray dog
scrabbling for scraps
in the unforgiving moonlight.

MAPPING THE MEGALOPOLIS

All day long we wheel and gawk
down avenues without end in the staggering City
bloated with makebelieve money
into a daunting colossus of urban sprawl
tumbling over the hills and up the gullies
ravenous megalopolis of concrete   glitter and kitsch
unwieldy Goliath of architectural overkill
living on speed   tomorrow's energy   borrowed time
in the ticking promise of the Fault

****

Across a spaghetti of freeways
that fling their coils in every direction but sanity
we ride through this heartland of films
bad luck   bad air   the flickering truths of dichotomy

****

Charlie Chaplin's gone from Sunset Strip
duckwalking away to tramp's heaven —
the tinsel gods are tarnished and dethroned
banished to three a.m. boxes and video tape
Fallen idols with fallen faces
even the craftiest surgeons can lift no more
hide behind lofty hedges in Beverly Hills
half-mummified in mansions
plagued by streetsmart punks who peddle their addresses
to a horde of tourists giddy with nostalgia

Hardened artery of Santa Monica Boulevard
home to secondrate restaurants   porno theatres
pawnshops   gay massage parlours
bankrupt jazzjoints   misfortune tellers
used carlots   used people lots, ribbons forever
across the City to the glum oil-rigged sea
and Venice Beach, lost to bohemian dreams
where angry bodybuilders hassle small black hustlers
bikers growl beerily in blues bars
overpriced boutiques pander to the trendy
belligerent panhandlers stem the likely
and jaded cops idle through an atmosphere
of obscure tension and holiday smog

East Fifth Street   the notorious *Nickel*
fouled and fermenting in the City's gut   garbage
ripe and piling in the gutters   wolfish
winos   junkies   crackheads   pillfreaks
lurching blindly through terminal scenarios
drowning in a sea of squalor and despair

Two harness bulls with pistols hauled
patting down two spreadeagled Chicanos
their palms flat against the bricks
like a scene from some t.v. crime flick

Vulturous pockmarked black face
framed in the broken curtainless
secondstory flophouse window
radiating sheer impotent hate

White chick with excruciating eyes
blank with drugs in a skull face
limping to no imaginable destination
beyond horror or help

Sunday on East Fifth Street

Rot at the Giant's heart

****

Across a spaghetti of freeways
that fling their strands over meanstreets growing meaner
we bear food and bottled water
back to our cheerful hosts in Pasadena

****

Southern subtropical night
drops down like a weight
We ride through a forest of lights
to a futuristic eight-storey mall
Outside escalators lift us through plexiglass tunnels
to a top-floor eighteen-theatre complex

The film is *Blade Runner*   it hurls us
one hundred years ahead   extrapolating the City
into what might well be should the world stand
and the trends continue   poisoned rain
falls endlessly on four-hundred storey monstrosities
each building a city in itself   Skycabs
hiss through polluted canyons
above abysmal streets where hired assassins
stalk renegade human clones
through a haunted hopeless future

Sated by grim images we descend
through the sciencefictional building
to the third-floor parking lot   empty save for us
and a lone Porsche in one corner

Suddenly the driverless car
begins to emit strident electronic beeps
like an endangered animal
Some thwarted prowler must have triggered
its alarm system   We exit hurriedly
before the cops arrive
Tomorrow is more than just around the corner
in this City gone out of control
where even empty cars cry out for help

****

Across a spaghetti of freeways
early next morning, we shake the City's traces
and flee its web of realities and myths
for Arizona and saner wide open spaces.

THE ANDY DEVINE ROOM

Kingman beyond the Mojave
sunbaked in old Arizona
wide dusty streets funnelling warm wind
1940 cafes full of professional characters
lazy garage where they retune our chariot
western museum with its sprawling mural
history evolving around the room
from geological obscurities
to the day before yesterday
an appropriate panorama
for this tidy old desert town dreaming of boom times
among the played-out mines

But this museum boasts something more unique
the Andy Devine Room
a shrine of filmic memorabilia
to Kingman's best-known son
photos review clippings   old movie posters
his modest celluloid legend
patchwork quilt of an actor's steady passage
flung across the walls for all to see

A montage of half-forgotten films
flashes unbidden across my mind
barrel-bellied slow-moving Andy
the hero's squeaky-voiced sidekick
in dozens of grade B backlot horse operas
joshing with John Wayne or Brian Donlevy
weathering sketchy scripts   indifferent directors
I can still hear that high-pitched raspy
bagpipe whinny of a laugh forever celebrating
the folly and money of it all

Now he dwells with the rest of them
in the twilight zone of the late late show
perennial character actor
always fifth or sixth in the billing
But not here in his hometown
in Kingman, Arizona
unassuming Andy Devine
will always be   a Star.

EL CANON GRANDE

Seven Cities of Cibola
Eldorados of infinite wealth
glimmering beyond the next horizon
somewhere in this land-without-end
Francisco Vasquez Coronado
driving his conquistadores
across harsh plains   treacherous rivers
cursing thirsting plodding doggedly on
beset by painted heathens among the trees
scraping graves in the alien dirt
in this year of our Lord 1540

Garcia Lopez de Cardenas
leading twelve men north
at Coronado's curt behest
to seek an indescribable wonder —
perhaps one of the golden cities —
hinted at in sign talk by friendly natives

Twenty hard-fought-days
up hard hills   through tangled forests
haunted by bear and wolf
climbing the climbing land
to an alpine plateau of wild meadows
grazing their mounts   soldiering on
threading through stands of scrub pine
without warning, almost stumbling
over the very edge of the Earth

Thirteen Spaniards spellbound —
El Canon Grande!
Mother of all abysses!
Words cannot capture this staggering rift
and they are warriors — not poets

The most daring attempt to descend
but reach impasse at the lower cliffs
clambering back to report that the mesas and buttes
seemingly manheight from far above
are taller in truth than even the tallest spires
of the Seville Cathedral

It is truly a marvel beyond marvels
their comrades will never believe them
but for all that, wryly muses
Garcia Lopez de Cardenas
it is still no golden city
stern Francisco Vasquez Coranado
will not be amused.

Breakdown On the South Rim

When we first stand
at the edge of that impossible ditch
all we can do is hopelessly laugh
at the sheer unalloyed ridiculous
enormity of it
God must have worn out a few shovels
when he dug this one

Getting a grip on ourselves
we commence the mandatory circuit
move from viewpoint to viewpoint
photographing each other
against guard rails on dizzy fingers of stone
with all the wind temples and wild castles
of torn Arizona
lifting out of that great gulf behind

At almost the final lookout
with the cliff-top tourist-trap village
the giddy mule trail below it
tilting across the precipice
the whole tree-capped river-carved chasm
snaking away to the Painted Desert
all reduced to one breathing postcard
whose only borders
are the limits of eyesight and mind,
the car blows its water hose
and leaves us marooned on the brink

After some realistic asessment
she hitchhikes into the village
leaving me to guard our stranded chariot
lest there be thieves in wonderland
Time trickles away
into that mile-deep trench
I pace between the dead car
and the dangerous allure of the drop
Shadows etch the North Wall
A chopper dragonflies over the buttes
An anxious hour passes and another
She doesn't return

The call of the Canyon fades to a whisper
in the clamor of mounting anxiety
It builds with orchestral insistence
What if by some perverse turn of luck
she hitched a ride with a psycho?
Hopelessly   helplessly
I realize how much I love her
and curse myself for not having gone
as apprehension ticks into alarm

Then just as I prepare
to abandon the expendable car
and set out in separate pursuit
the most welcome tow-truck
I ever saw in my life
comes wheeling like magic around the bend

"They close the garage for lunch," she says
giving me that smile
that could light up a neon sign
and at that infinitely thankful moment I know
she is more singular and marvelous to me
than all the wonder of all the Grand Canyon
yawning huge and inconsequential
under the sun.

THE SUN FALLS OVER THE EDGE OF KANSAS

Night blows like smoke
across the patterned flatland
gold fires the horizon
the sun falls over the edge of Kansas

Time slows to an odd crawl
at the outskirts of Dodge City
it moves away from us like a mirage
the car creeps through remembering shadows

Here in a trail-town sprung from an army camp
in the turmoil of another century
the Old West paused for a moment
to count her rabble   sort out her heroes

These are the precincts of legend
Wyatt Earp rode through this same dusk
Bat Masterson tested his gunhand here
Doc Holliday coughed from bottle to bottle

Here were the archetypes forged
in the dust of a harsher reality
not guessing their ghosts would surge forth
to fuel a million sagebrush fantasies

But what of the town today?
Vainly I try to envision it
as we inch through endless minutes
across that time-warped plain

After eternity — Dodge
it flaunts its modernity at us
brighter with neon than prairie moonlight
a city like any other city

But it has its peculiarities
we know where we are by the names
Earp Burgers   Masterson Laundromats
they do right by their gunslingers here

And they've tossed up a shrine to their heroes
a cardboard street with a Longbranch Saloon
where they only serve soda pop
and thirsty Doc Holiday scowls from his photograph

In the historical museum
James Arness and Errol Flynn
share equal billing with Masterson's six-gun
they honor the fictions along with the facts

In a recreated Boot Hill
on the edge of the actual graveyard
we stand in a garden of sardonic epitaphs
but no bones lie below those headboards

The Old West in Dodge
has been packaged like a commodity
the town spins like a slow-motion twister
sucking the tourists into its vortex

Number us gladly among them
tonight we will feast on Texas toast
and the best damn steaks in America
served by a girl with a southern drawl

and tired with road's-end joy
we will fall to our rented bed
and dream all night of dichotomous Dodge
till the sun climbs over the edge of Kansas

PAWNEE ROCK

Fields of dead sunflowers
rank upon rank of shrivelled parasols
an army of scarecrows in the sun
Country so flat   long-farmed   predictable
even the car stifles a yawn
Old bloodstained land
tamed   apportioned   at peace
a scatter of interchangeable towns
grain elevator outposts of Middle America
hugging the highway   the train tracks
in dead-level stretching monotony

Enigmatic literature at a turnoff:
Pawnee Rock   National Monument   One Half Mile
No evidence of any such promontory
It warrants looking into

Sure enough beyond sparse trees
Pawnee Rock   or rather
what's left of it   a mere molehill now
the bulk of it blasted to rubble
shovelled away by gandy dancers
for rail-bed fill in the track-laying years —
its original height simulated
by an apologetic lookout tower

Atop that high platform in the wind
we gaze out over the checkerboard prairie
thinking of wagon trains   Indian raids
cattle wars   barn-raising bees
and how Pawnee Rock
is a dead-apt   ironic metaphor
for the whole lost West

STUNNED WITH HIGHWAYS

Stunned with highways
we chase the ghost of a gangster
across the epic belly of America
through cattlecall wastelands
past geronimo mesas
over mountain passes in sidewinding winds

Stunned with highways
where distant perspectives of blacktop
mirage into mirrors
through which great semis plunge
actually casting reflections
in the illusory looking-glass hardtop
that always melt into desert air
long before we reach them

Stunned with highways
strung like tightwires between horizons
leaping legendary rivers
lazy Mississippi   wide Missouri
bridging the famous places
bluesy Kansas City   racingmad Indianapolis
in a tangled confusion of branches
that always resolve to a single freeway again
on the other side

Stunned with highways
the endless Kerouacian Road
roping everywhere and anywhere
lined with exploded tires   dead animals
we chase the ghost of a gangster
across the epic belly of America.

NIGHT MANOEVRES

In a silent barn of war
in a rainy Ontario meadow the death-wagons sleep
strange stock for a farm to harbour
tank and howitzer
gun carriage   armoured car
and a mobile command-post once used by General Crerar

The collector has magicked them here
with a wave of his money-wand —
he tends to their fractures   oils their rusty works
a curious exercise
to husband a herd of life-size Dinky Toys —
it is like a boyhood hobby gone berserk

At night when the field is still
and the shepherd of ordinance deep in his martial dreams
something stirs in the barn like mice in a sack —
the battered command-post glows and there they are —
dapper Montgomery   moustached mournful Crerar
and unflappable Churchill sipping his cognac

The old expenders of blood
the crafty chess-lords of carnage juggling lives
they foddered the cannons well when the years ran red
now they are met again
like ominous echoes to mount a phantom campaign
to sift the unquiet ashes of battle and summon the dead

The orders are given and heard
the locked barn doors swing wide
the ragtag force rolls forth   an army reborn
to scour this war-spared land
to the dimly-remembered whim of an old command
and hunt for ghostly panzer divisions till dawn

GARDEN OF RUINS

In the Gatineau Hills
William Lyon Mackenzie King
not to anyone's particular surprise
planted a garden of ruins
to amuse himself between seances

At considerable expense
various balustrades, columns and bricks
were brought here from great distances
to assume a new surreal function
in this picturebook place he called Kingsmuir

In a vaulting amputated doorway
that once belonged to a bank
and now leads nowhere forever
we pose like materializing spacefarers
just beamed down from a starship

Over an abbeylike ivied ruin
that might always have been here
but was actually carried piecemeal from England
small boys climb like excited monkeys
making a bilingual chatter

It is a Daliesque landscape
eeccentric as the man who bequeathed it
and I imagine I glimpse him briefly
small   scant-haired   morning-suited   sad
strolling obliviously among the Sunday tourists

TORONTO THE MOIST

Earle Birney, my love and I
wandering Toronto in the rain
after coffee
in his twenty-second floor aerie
(entirely appropriate roost
for an old mountain scrambler}
good conversation
of poetry   falls from trees   Holy Herb Wilson
and the faraway westcoast
where Dylan Thomas and Malcolm Lowry
once collided again like two floundering ships
under Earle's aegis

Bowls of thick goulash soup
in a Hungarian restaurant
{poor Earle intending to treat
but forgetting his wallet —
later sending a record as recompense}
and now scouring soaking-wet streets
for our mislaid station-wagon
playing hide and seek with us
through a maze of maple trees
in that unknown neighbourhood

My love and Earle
talking familiarly of South America
riots   tear-gas   poverty   Fascism —
me, travel-novice, mostly listening
to exotic yarns of Uruguay and Peru
our minds sliding
over the curve of the world
far from windy   besquirreled
unromantic Toronto
our elusive station-wagon
and the slow drenching rain.

THE CAPITAL OF BREAKFAST

Quite early one morning
we rattle into Battle Creek
in Michigan's breadbasket
a thoroughly apt hour
to arrive at this seat of cereals —
a town that grew famous on Snap   Crackle   Pop

For two who were raised
in the rank effluvia of pulpmill towns
this place is a fragrant surprise
Entering Battle Creek
is like driving back into childhood
through the mouth of a king kong sized
Corn Flakes box

Curious over the town's name
we rummage through the local records
but there is no mention of any battle
famous or otherwise
"Judging by the number of overweight people around here
they could be talking about
the Battle of the Bulge," you observe

The only hint of possible excitement
around Battle Creek
is the Tornado Shelter sign
on the Public Library
but I suppose you might tend
to get a bit bland
if you'd spent most of your life
inhaling soporfic aromas of Puffed Rice and Grape Nuts
wafting eternally from the cereal factories
in the Capital of Breakfast

PASTY LAND

Over a long and low-slung bridge
that straddles the strait between Great Lakes
in windy northern Michigan
we cross the threshhold of Pasty Land

Here the ubiquitous burger stands
the immemorial chicken snacks
the hot-dog vendors   the taco joints
have been upstaged by a different snack

The signboards pepper both sides of the road
Jean's Pasties   Queen's Pasties
(with unlikely visions of Royal Liz
doing a decorous bump and grind)
Guido's Pasties   Moishe's Pasties
(do they serve kosher and pizza pasties?)
Wing's Pasties   Singh's Pasties
The mind fairly boggles in Pasty Land

That night in a lakehead bed
I dream of a mythical Cornishman
moving like Johnny Appleseed
resolute over the countryside
scattering pasties in his wake
spreading the creed of his favorite feed
zealot-eyed through the Michigan mist
a full-blown pasty evangelist.

THE GUNMEN OF NORTH DAKOTA

Through the morning diner
the gunmen of North Dakota
stalk like shock troops
in their camouflage jackets —
good old boys from the bad old days

They've parked their rifles
in pickups outside
now they crowd a commandeered table
and hold a war council
involving the undoing of ducks

They're going shooting in the sloughs
innocent hunters
out to stock their freezers
Why do their faces have
that certain sly suggestion of menace?

They pay us no mind whatsoever
deep in talk of blinds and decoys
Why is there a hint
.of something else in their voices —
a certain sinister undertone?

Somehow I'm glad these are no longer
the psychedelic Sixties
and you and I, my love, two hapless hippies
in a technicolor   sittingduck
Volkswagen van.

ONE OLD SOREHEAD

After a hundred innoccuous announcements
for one-horse one-bar no-towns
that don't even rate a microdot on the map
the small red billboard
jumps up out of the buffalo grass
like a glad shout of surprise

596 Nice People it announces
and One Old Sorehead
We're riproaring
and raring to for business! —
the most intriguing sign we've seen
in 16 States and three Provinces

It stops us in our tracks
We detour to check the place over
Any town with the sheer gumption
to hang out a shingle like that
has to be more than your average
common-or-garden whistle-stop

Instant letdown   The place lounges
moribund beside the tracks   broken-windowed
boarded-up stores   gutted gas stations
closedforever cafes   bankrupt banks
gone-all-to-hell hotels   a chickencoop post office
one live saloon with two customers

"Looks to me,"you say
"as though the old sorehead must have had
the last laugh around here"
And we tool off through Montana realizing
that you can't ever judge a book by its cover
or a town by its sign.

WE MEASURE THE MILES IN MUFFETS

Laughing our way through Wisconsin
we measure the miles in Muffets
for so you have christened the hay bundles
that throng the the mown fields
as though newly tumbled
from some celestial cereal box in the sky

Round and perfect as yellow cheeses
they stock the pastures
dwindling into the distance
to become dime-sized in remote farmlands
benign and cheerful in sunlight
sinister somehow at twilight
like great waiting wheels
ready to roll upon us

How we disparage the drab spreads
where the hay is bundled in mundane rectangles
or piled in loaves like so much bread
Only the Muffets win our approval
like old friends   happy omens
they guide us across the top of America

Bending up out of Montana
through ugly towns with beautiful names
Sweetwater   Sunburst
we cross the line and find to our pleasure
more of our mute companions —
the Muffets have trundled to Canada too

Now in a bright niche of memory
the Muffets shine like gold coins
a currency of droll magic
that bought us a bushel of wonders
in the fall of a travelling year
in the warm fall of our lives.

DROWNED RENATA

It was an Eden-like place
of dusty roads   bees and busy farmers
of cherry trees alive with drowsy birds
dreaming in the breeze of fruitful summers

It grew from a single lakeside hotel
for wayfaring silver miners
but a man named Dobbs and his loyal horse, Jack
were the town's true founders

Dobbs was a kindly caring man
a poet   a good neighbour
he wrote Jack's epitaph when his old companion died
now their bones lie close together

From every compass point the settlers came
to work the fertile ground
to raise homesteads and children by the lake
as the seasons waxed and waned

Around these simple beginnings
the town took shape and prospered
In due course the ugly name was changed
from Dog Creek to Renata

Renata is Spanish for *Rebirth*
It was an ironic choice
In 1968 the B.C.Hydro
dammed the Columbia River
and raised the Arrow Lakes

The lifting inexorable waters
drew Renata under
the fields   orchards   evacuated homes
the sawmill   the stores   the swimming beaches
the packing house   the churches
disappeared forever

Nothing remains today of drowned Renata
but a lonely schoolhouse on a benchland
a cemented-over graveyard
the cherry blossoms no longer blow
and only schools of curious fish
follow the ghosts of old Dobbs and his horse
along those sunken country roads

BIRDPORT

Like a fallen cloud
the snow geese carpet the acres-wide slough
in a monumental gaggle
wall-to-wall honkers hunkering down
in the marshmud
of this millennial way station

Ice and instinct
have triggered this autumn exodus
directed them here
in arrowhead formations
On these flats long-fertilized
with ancestral droppings
they have dropped in feathered squadrons
to rest their wings   refuel
forage   gossip   take a familiar breather
on the long lift south

No random gunshots
will thin their ranks
in this protected place
legacy of a bird-loving rum-runner
Soon they will climb the air again
resume their instinctive flight patterns
leaving the refuge to less-adventuresome fowl
woodpeckers   flickers   starlings
seagulls   ravens   occasional eagles
and the dabbling caretaker ducks.

SERPENTINE FEN

Pocket of beauty locked between parallel highways
fringed by farmfields —
protected marsh with the sinuous name
chittering with birdsong under the sun

Serpentine River, true to its calling
snakes across the northern margins —
silty oceanic channel, toothed with oysters
flooding coffee-coloured below the dike

This is an avian eden now —
a metropolis of bullrushes
where small things flit through seedrich aisles
celebrating summer's rebirth

Redwinged blackbirds crimson the thickets —
a trusting mother duck parades her brood —
swallows loft to nests in rickety lookout towers —
killdeer glide like brown phantoms over the dike path

Larger birds throng the southern reaches —
families of geese flotilla the quiet sloughs —
great blue heron   aloof   inscrutable
stands guard among a cluster of tiny islands

The frail old man of the marsh
perennial watcher of Serpentine Fen
reclines on a shooting stick
blue-veined hands clutching a high-powered telescope

His failing eyes are intent
as he studies the bird-busy swamp —
ancient amid the joy   the regeneration
he savours this yearly ritual

"Two California avocets are nesting here
for the first time," he quavers
alight with the wonder of it   and somehow
that small marvel seems far more significant
than all the crimes and crises
that yammer hysterically forever
beyond this sanctuary.

THE FLEDGLINGS

Eagerly under the beckoning sky
they have gathered at China Creek Park
incongruous splash of green at the City's centre
surrounded by industrial temples   wasteground
with Sky Trains shuddering by through the distance
to take their first winged and stumbling runs
fledgling hang-gliders flinging themselves
down grassy slopes   hungering
for the wind's lifting fingers

They have time in their pockets   they tingle
they lust for the heights
On this first and fumbling day
they strap on the great coloured wings
rush again and again down the tilt of the hill
courting flight like a dangerous lover

Not all
will achieve their giddy dreams
Some will experience second thoughts
when they stand at last on the daunting summits
of Sumas Mountain   Woodside or Vedder
with half the Fraser Valley
twenty-five hundred feet below
ant cars   toy buildings   lilliputian fields
laid out like an aerial photograph

But most will straddle the challenge
swallow their qualms   move in turn to the ramp
check their harnesses   shudder   shrug   run
leap off the edge of the world
offer themselves and their wings to the wind
loft unbelieving over the patterned land
leaving their earth-selves behind.

The Birdpeople and the Birds

They have entered a realm
already inhabited
by those who were born winged
They study the interlopers
with glittering inquisitive eyes

The birds
fear the roaring things   the yammering giants
who have thundered through their kingdom for decades
these new ones are different
they swoop silently
though their wings do not beat
they do not trouble the air with their shouts
they seek only
the lifting places

The birds
do not fear the newcomers
they have limbs and faces
their alienness is a cousinly thing
that can be lived with
Sometimes
the sparrows fly in the shadow of their wings
the swifts guide them to thermals
even the fierce proud eagles
aloofly salute them

Only the red-tufted hawks
have no tolerance
for the quiet kite people
Fired by some irrational hate
they dive pettishly at the hang-gliders
shrilly harass them   at their angriest
fly upsidedown beneath them
talons extended belligerently

going for the eyes

MOTH DANCE

That uncertain morning
after the all-night party
his caution off-kilter with beer and smoke
he gives the finger to better judgement
scoffs in the face of advice
ties on his wings like an unsteady condor
kicks from the mountain top

Now he is truly godlike
more wild with flight than ever before
butterfly-free, he planes through the currents
daring the air to unseat him
whooping his joy to the spinning world

If he could chase down a thermal
he would swim to its lifting core
climb it like Jacob's Ladder
halfway to heaven and higher
But the day is too young   the rocks
are hoarding their heat like batteries
the updrafts are sleeping   the sky
is still as milk

His time will be brief   soon he will sink
he must ride the moment
swooping above the treetops, he spots the snag
gnarled   windshook   spike-topped   dead
fingering grey from the green

It draws him like a flame   the dance begins
a game of aerial chicken
He toys with the dead tree, taunting it
buzzing it with ever-tightening passes
reckless matador of the melting day

But fatigue has stolen his edge
his instincts are blunted — he swoops too close ||
One wing catches the snag — it tears and buckles
he drops like a stone.
His body shattered he lies
at the dead tree's foot
cast by his folly
forever out of the sky.

Blue Thermal

Somewhere it rises, that vast invisible chimney
mother of updrafts
elevator to infinity gusting skyward
born of heat and barren ground
cloudthruster taller than time
tunnel to the air's summit

Those who saddle the wind
dream of that perfect thermal
blue skyshaft to elsewhere
in visions it clasps their wings with sure hands
like sparks from a bonfire they spin
riding its lift to ultimate altitudes

Higher than height they spiral
lost to all griefs and gravities
into a new state of being
altered   exalted
one with the fickle element
at last

DEMOLITION DERBY

Impatient steel beasts,
the war-painted cars poise for battle
grinding their gears like teeth —
pawing the dirt with their wheels —
come from far and near
to this fairground field of ritual combat

The starting flag unleashes them —
gunning their motors they spring to the clash —
thumping bumping battering
buckling fenders rupturing grilles
round and round they shudder and snort
in a dance of rattling mayhem

The air grows rank with scorching rubber —
the cars joust on through smoke and steam —
mad mechanical knights
One by one
overstressed engines give up the ghost —
wheezing wearily limp to a halt

At last only two combatants are left —
a seemingly-unscathed white sedan —
an orange van almost hammered to scrap
The odds seem stacked in the white car's favour
but the old orange beater refuses to yield —
again and again it limps back like a gallant boxer

The crowd begins to chant and cheer
urging the mobile junkheap on
Finally the underdog, its forward gear gone
its wheels askew   its tires ripped to ribbons
summons the last of its courage   grates into reverse —
slams the white sedan into final submission

The delighted crowd explodes —
we join in the standing ovation —
leave the bleachers amazed
to have actually found an uplifting emotion
in something so gratuitously violent
as a demolition derby.

IN THE PEACEABLE KINGDOM

How to write about something
of such elusive charm
that the simple beauty of it
almost beggars description?

"It's just for kids," I protested
but she convinced me it wasn't
so at the end of a pleasure-crammed day
we entered the Petting Zoo

In the fenced compound
the eager animals clustered around us —
geese of equable temperament —
guileless baby goats —
a somewhat bewildered bull calf —
a delegation of rabbits   a courtly llama
a small black sheep who shyly pawed at my leg

We bought cones of green meal
to feed the trusting beasts
and moving among children
both animal and human
briefly became children too

Evening tip-toed through the pavilion
as we took our leave —
the llama lay down with the calf
in peaceable brotherhood —
it was as though we had touched a memory of Eden
for a strange and magical moment.

BARKERVILLE CAT

The cat
comes mewing welcome at us through the chill
a small custodian
the only dweller in this hollow town

The season's done
the minstrels and the dancing girls are gone
the tourists tan
on southern beaches now   the ghosts return

The cat
scurries before us down forsaken streets
leading us on
past dead saloons   cold smithies   shuttered banks

Sometimes he vanishes
then like a conjured rabbit reappears
a grey familiar
a sole survivor in this vacant place

The cat
stays surely with us as we make our rounds
watches us wanly as we take our leave
then pads back to the ghost town   darts inside
and lies in wait for more late guests to guide

HOCKEY POEM

Poems are something
like hockey players
nurtured in the junior leagues
the farm teams of the subconscious

Every so often
you advance them to the majors
hoping
they'll make the grade for you
score literary goals
deke the critics
When they don't come up to snuff
you ship them
back down to the minors

Always
you draw more culls than champions
sometimes useful workhorses
who can't skate
sometimes dazzling skaters
who can't score
Gingerly
you juggle your lines
assemble your teams
All too often
they don't even make the playoffs

But a poet
is like a patient coach
The game
must go on
After every defeat
you lick your wounds
study the mental draft choices
always on the lookout
for a Gretsky.

A BEATING LIKE MEDICINE DRUMS

The story shudders yet
through Nishga lore —
is told on totem poles throughout this country
of how the Gods
angered by young braves
who turned their backs on old tradition
killing small animals for sport alone —
tormenting salmon
with burning pitch-pine splinters
turning them into living torches,
decreed a fiery judgement
for their careless cruelty

The ghosts awoke —
there was a beating in the ground
like medicine drums
growing ever louder —
rising to a thunderous cacophany
till the mountains burst open
gouting flame and smoke —
over the shaking land —
igniting the forest —
engulfing the villages —
cremating many Nishga —
putting the rest to terrified flight

When the fury subsided
the course of the Nass River had been altered —
new lakes had been created —
the land was changed forever

Three hundred years later
the scars have scarcely healed —
we ride through this place of old ruin —
fourteen miles of hardened magma —
walls and hummocks of distorted black slag
like the aftermath of a nuclear war —
carpeted with green lichen
slowly eating the lava away

But it will be centuries yet
before the grim signature
of the enraged Gods is erased —
before the beating of medicine drums
dies finally away
from this disasterstruck and punished land

THE CORKSCREW TREES OF KITSELAS

The corkscrew trees of Kitselas
twist up from the primeval moss
of the ancient forest
as though two giant hands
had wrung them like dishrags

Strange trees
coiling like brown Narwhal horns
towards the thin October sun —
anomalies of nature
among their arrow-straight cousins

Yet fitting symbols somehow
for this curious country
where black bears wear white coats
ancient lava flows wear blankets of green lichen
and the old hills wear history like a ceremonial robe

PAINTED DREAMS ON HAIDA GWAAI

The weather flickers crazily here
to fickle Pacific whims
Rainbows arch brilliant in the sun
ribbons of colour leaping up among the eagles
from bogs and log dumps
to fade like painted dreams in sudden sun

This is a place of painted dreams —
spectral images that fluctuate   flood and fade
slipping in and out of thought
Haida in their pride and prime
monarchs of the heaving coastal waters
striking weaker mainland villages without warning
paddling home with slaves and plunder
to their sea-locked kingdom

Painted dreams
on time's shifting canvas —
ancestral settlements
abandoned in the smallpox plague —
roofless lodges
topless house posts
moss-furred unfinished canoes
totems rotting wanly in the rain —
proud warrior people
conquered by an alien germ

Painted dreams
of ancient
indecipherable petroglyphs
enigmatic on sea rocks
carved by unknown artisans
of some forgotten race
long before the Haida
claimed these mist-kept islands

Painted dreams
of first white settlers
raising cabins
in hazy clearings —
the loggers who followed them
to roar like hungry dragons in the hills
with saws and donkey engines
plundering primeval forests —
strewing devastation in their wake —
caulk-booted conquistadores
riding roughshod
across the untrammelled land

Painted dreams on Haida Gwaai
where past and present intertwine
like filaments
of some unseen web
holding us captive
in threads of legend —
strands of sad history —
meshes of magic

PEACE RIVER WHITEOUT
for Yvonne

We must have brought winter back with us
to that Big Sky land beyond the mountains
or else it had seen us coming —
northern novices bouncing over the frost heaves
through Pine Pass —
and wanted to give us a taste
of sub-arctic hospitality

For weeks the country had flowered
in false El Nino spring —
the usual cold had seemingly retreated
Now the weather's wheel turned back suddenly —
Heaven's blue eye cataracted over —
a persnickety wind flailed down from the north —
the clouds collapsed into wet whirling pieces —
the world reverted to blizzardly limbo

On that raised road there was no turning off
we could only crawl on through the shattered day
hammered by upstart gusts and gales —
blinded by freezing confetti

"Maybe we're just a couple of mistakes
Nature's trying to white out"
she joked nervously

I imagined God
with a Deity-sized bottle of Liquid Paper
trying to expunge us
from the smudged pages of history —
somehow
it really wasn't all that funny

Behind us
an enormous semi bulked out of the blur
a lumbering nemesis
dogging our tracks

Mercifully
the road widened briefly —
the truck shouldered past us —
we hugged its tail like a bird dog —
kept our wheels in its comforting tracks —
passed it in turn as the snow curtain thinned
till we broke all at once from frightening white
into startling sunlight
elated   recreated
unerased

BREAKFAST IN THE PORTAL COUNTRY

In this Peace River valley
the wind stirs echoes of other times —
paddle-splash and song
phantom canoes muscling their way upstream —
tireless voyageurs with bearded faces
breaking trails beyond the mountains
to the beavered wilds of New Caledonia

This was the portal country —
first hard pathway to the Pacific
opened by Alexander Mackenzie
followed by John Finlay   Simon Fraser —
argonauts of the white water
braving hostile Natives   drunk with exploration —
driven by burning dreams of pelts and profit

But the fur brigades have faded into history —
their bastioned forts have fallen   rotted   vanished —
the hunter's muskets bark no more along the Peace —
the rugging and the moving times are done —
the long slaughter is long over —
the beaver sleep unthreatened in their lodges

At a truck-stop cafe
two burly Native drivers
sporting gold necklaces   earrings
park their rigs outside   find an empty booth
josh with the waitress   order coffees   study the menu
"Those are the new voyageurs" you say.

The Sacked Forsaken Places

Across that riverbank meadow
the time-greyed cabins sprawl like broken dreams
of yesterday occasions   high times long struck low
by the slow mallets of the years
artifacts of otherday endeavours
scattered to the wheeling weather
shadowed by skeletal tree arms
haunting as half-forgotten songs
testaments to mortality
in the museum light of morning

Here at the rustling forks
where the Quesnel and Cariboo Rivers
mingle and meld like lovers
in watery conjunction
loveless miners raised this ragged town
to roar its moment glory
in the yellow name of gold
When the boom years passed it flickered on
Industrious Chinese
kept the dimming flame alight —
worked the worked-out creeks —
wintered and wandered   dallied the days away
until their last Mah Jong tiles
clicked into silence
They inhabit
a quieter village now —
the white-crossed graveyard
that broods beside these ruins

Such ghost towns
strew the deserted hinterlands —
monuments to yesterday —
bastions of vanished hopes
sacked forsaken places.

OCTOBER RAFTS ON FRASER'S RIVER

Corsetted in life jackets
we clamber awkwardly
aboard the bobbing river rafts
with their rubber pontoons
like giant trussed-together sausages,
a motley mostly-nervous crew of history buffs
committed to run the feisty Fraser

Casting off from Boston Bar
we drift away downstream
a gang of old and young
Huckleberry Finns
but this is no placid Mississippi cruise
we are embarking upon

History haunts through our heads —
this is the same rambunctious flood
that drove Simon Fraser
to clamber the cliffs
along spidery Native trapezes
slung from the upper bluffs —
to swing outward dangerously
with only wet hazards gnashing below —
to drop back to the dripping rock face —
to sigh with relief on the other side

This is no casual millstream
we have chosen to adventure down —
this thunderous waterway
has swallowed men without mercy —
the first rapids pummel us —
the rafts bend and buck like maverick horses

October hurries us
along the frothing pathways of legend —
fish-eye viewpoints of the canyon —
grotesque current-carved sculptures
invisible from above
loom surreally around us

We gird ourselves for Hell's Gate
the narrow notorious river-throat
that stymied Fraser's flimsy canoes
It seems to be overrated —
at least at this low water —
two enormous thwacking belly-flops
soak us with spray   then we're through —
two subsequent stretches of turbulence
will prove much wilder than this

Three hours we ride the currents
save for a brief landfall at Spuzzum —
by the time we beach in Yale
half frozen from toppling temperatures
we can think only of hot baths —
shedding our bulky straightjackets
we scuttle gladly to cars,
homebound journeyfolk
of the boisterous fall torrents.

Rainbow's-End Horizons

It was the luck of our love
that guided us through those magical journeys -
two of us twinned together   yondering
through the unwinding wonder of the land

Over the hills and far afield
we sailed through star-crossed dreams -
how I loved you and love you still
gentle companion of all those shimmering distances

Darby and Joan in the making
we sang ourselves happy to unknown outports -
nothing could mar or sully our joy -
we lived our wishes   tasted the wine of the sunset

Jubilant children of the wind
we smiled through a glow of togetherness -
anywhere-seekers, drunk with the thrill of away
we lofted like happy birds to those far-flung places

Time perhaps has spiked our wheels -
the wanderlust years are consigned to memory
but the luck of our love lives on   our souls still sing -
the myth of our comings and goings will never die

Darkness cannot erase those glad recollections -
age can never diminish those glittering odysseys -
along the heart's secret highways we'll travel forever
towards those beckoning rainbow's-end horizons.

LOVE STORY
for Yvonne

To hold you in the night
is my joy and longing
to feel the pulse of your being
in the warm shape of a woman
to know a light in my loneliness
a strength in our melding

Dim ages ago
our mothers foresaw the truth of us
knew that our lives could blend
into an ease   a rightness
but I was poisoned with ignorance
and would not listen   could not love

Down dark squandered years
I reeled like a drunken ghost
living only a travesty of life
blind as a cave cricket
while you moved beautiful beyond me
in the orbit of another man's world

But the bolts were drawn in the end
the impossible came to be
you clasped me to your sanity
and gave me sanity
the fog parted at last
I saw true wonder catch fire in your eyes

There is nothing new in this
it is a story older than song
and there is much of singing in it
you are my love and my meaning
To hold you in the night
is my joy and longing.

THE UNDERCOUNTRY

Darkness speaks like a stinging thing
when the scales tip from sanity
into the negative drifts —
the caves of deceit and misdirection

Under the safe levels of love
there is another place
where something laughs   a venal clown
wearing my face like a mask

On this wrong side of the mirror
all the old demons are still dancing
widdershins in thin pent light —
they have not been exorcised   they are waiting

All the regressive memories
coil like poisonous snakes
in the bitterest pits of the mind —
their venom is just as deadly as ever

My darkness speaks like a stinging thing —
I will not heed its voice —
I will slam the lid on the beckoning demons
and move again to the levels of love

BALANCING ACT
A Song For Yvonne

Cut-out trees inkblot the sky
on a wan day with a stormfront weeping
over and in from the devious sea
night is resculpting the face of the world
summer has drained back into the future
I crouch on the edge of a bottomless pit
only my love for you keeps me from falling

Sing an old song, sad as a cripple
sunlight has sidled away like a dream
soapsud hope spins quick down the drainpipe
ghosts of uncertainty grope from the curtains
quicksand time is sucking me down
nothing rings right in this drumbeating gloom
only my love for you keeps me from failing

Soon I will climb a mountain of tricks
back to your truth through screes of confusion
claw up the slopes with fingers like thumbs
nothing but trust to spur my ascent
but you will be there   you will be there
the knowing's a drug that will sustain me
over the ledges   along the crests
to your wide warm eyes   your warm wide arms
your soft safe body   your dear bright voice
only our love will keep me from failing
only our love will keep me from falling.

THE DWINDLING

Fading peach sky slides
behind dusty dusk mountains —
firststar hangs pinned
to pale blue
that widens and climbs
to indigo —
grease sea breathes away
its last silver —
filagree trees flex
silhouette fingers   pull
darkness to them   gradually
vanish —
night fills the hedged
world within the garden —
green flees —
townlights twitch alive
where the lost
sea stops —
fireplace
crackles awake —
your dark head rests
vital against my shoulder —
the universe
reduces to a room

THE WALTZ OF WHAT YOU ARE

In the waltz of what you are
the dreams shimmer and shift
wishwoman
you gleam strong through my stupidity

Dark and light of our wonderful madness
in a moil of sheets
shipwrecked on your breasts
when the world's a wisdom we take or leave

The alchemy of our love —
the trading of truths —
it took so long to kindle —
now it burns with a clear light

When we laugh together
it is always morning   the sun comes up in your eyes
this is our private country   we lock like spoons
in a touching of more than flesh

You are my more-than-love —
my life's great luck   my life —
dance with me sweetheart as I dream,
through the waltz of what you are

ELIZABETHAN LOVE DANCE
for Yvonne

Prettily step, my changeling, my darling
coalescing born to caress
out of the muddle of masks and charades —
warm for the touching tender to kiss
Infinite strangeness of burgeoning love
quick in the soul like a gull upflung —
silken as roseflesh heady as honeywine
private as breathing lovely as song

Love, we have walked the ways of perplexment
touching and parting too much apart —
seeking from others the quicksilver tingle —
wandering lost in the woods of the heart —
spiralling down through whirlpool illusions —
spinning so close then drifting away —
prisoned in distances clasping in mirrors —
night dreams of tenderness lost to the day

Faltering altering reaching retreating
sparring words awkwardly, tense and remote —
breathing adieu in bars and at funerals —
always unsatisfied never complete
Yet there is something that builds with each leaving —
strengthens in loneliness profits from loss —
richens from wrangling outlives uncertainty —
beckons us closer for better or worse

Now with your coming, you magic my morning —
I hold your face in my mind like a star —
I hear the voice that whispers and wins me —
I clasp you dearly   I treasure you more
Prettily step, my changeling, my darling
coalescing   born to caress
out of the muddle of masks and charades
warm for the touching   tender to kiss.

My Thoughts Swim After You
for Yvonne

As you drift away from me up the Coast
into adventures I cannot share
I yearn for the song of you
that magicked me into a whole person
when we laughed together
on the best days I have ever known

There was strain in our parting —
a painful edgy awakwardness
it cuts me to recall —
words turned inadequate —
a stiff and bitter silence
dropped between us

On this warm uncertain afternoon
my thoughts swim after you
up the Inside Passage —
my ghost hand caresses your hair —
my ghost mouth brushes your lips —
my ghost arms close around you

Once, years ago, you moved away from me
down the windy reaches of Long Beach
before I had learned to walk with you
Then you returned and began to teach me
all the special secrets of your being
It was the first real lesson of my life

Come back to me again, my darling
along that profounder beach
that is the rest of our lives
You are my only true companion —
my love beyond all other loves
We have walked the weathers
hand in hand
I have forgotten
how to walk alone.

I Used to Sing to my Chokermen

I used to sing to my chokermen
on impossible hills when the rain stung down —
when the fog marched up like an army of ghosts
and the sky was the colour of sorrow

It was then I sang to my chokermen
making a game of our mountainside plight —
setting a tune to our workaday dance
while the wind whipped round and the trees wept

Now I sing safe in the mystery of love
reprieved from those long-ago labours —
I wake to the warmth of a tender touch —
the hardscrabble years are behind me

But somehow I sing to my chokermen yet
for life is an endless conundrum —
somewhere I leap down the hills of my youth
in a dream of yesterday's music

Those are just fancies that come in the night —
time has abducted my chokermen —
daily I sing in the key of love —
the past fades away like a figment.

FOUND MY LADY

Found my lady
after all those empty years
wit-strapped and spooked
in funless fun houses
beside beer rivers
wine lakes
whiskey seas —
sucking potsmoke
in acid anti-establishments —
knowing only
paper-thin relationships —
almost-but-not-quite romances —
skewed antagonistic friendships —
hunched drunkenly
in smoky book-crammed rooms
to the clamour of scratchy records —
disjointed conversation
yammering at cross purposes
through the confusion —
cockeyed   quixotic   neurotic
touch-no-bases times —
no one to really talk to —
no one to honestly love —
cracked as an egg on rubber-legged mornings

That was how it went
down the years of delerium
lost among unlike-minded strangers
drinking in senseless rhythm with me —
trying to be friends —
out of sync with my eccentricities —
not my people

But time, thankfully, has a way
of segueing into rightness
After decades of false turns and fallacies —
after so many mismatches and mistakes —
after oceans of alcohol   countries of drugs
found my purpose
found my soulmate
found my lady.

MY LOVE WHO WALKS IN MAGIC

In the dearest times you become your smile
you scintillate beauty through all gaps and gulfs
all barriers   all lies   all fears

It is the wisest warmest look
I have ever known or dreamed
It draws me like a lamp from the spider recesses

You are the sanest softest girl I have ever lingered with
you breathe your life with a fierce joy
you absorb your world in all its accents and essences

You know the true metre of time
you treasure your days like rare coins
you glory in minor keys   dewdrop jewels and small things dancing

You are a student of stars and winds
people   birds   the language of waves
the structures of hope   the rhythms of wishing

In the dearest times you become your smile
your eyes
kiss the blindness from mine
I see for a little as you see always

Unbelieving   unworthy
I move to your arms like a tranced man
my love who lives with more true poetry
than I have ever written or dreamed.

A SMALL HUM OF JOY IN THE HEART
for Yvonne

In the prickly darkness
I prowl the rim of consciousness
tracking a lost sensibility
hidden behind the forebrain
in thickets of memory —
twisting away   disappearing
around blind corners of the cortex

I spin through dither and dream
to the ghostplace
where poems once shivered alive —
tingled and twitched   initiating
a small hum of joy in the heart

I scrabble back
to old creative days
when the good poems danced with the bad
in prolific confusion —
splashed in the pools of my being —
coddled in the blithers —
whistled in the fiff —
gibberish of undecoded poetry
before it became poetry
shrugging itself lucid —
forming itself into ranks —
marching away to the fingertips

But the poems sift slow now   infrequently —
the fluency has forsaken me —
the sturdiest verses were nurtured in loneliness —
perhaps love has bred a complacency

Love is a lotus song   an exquisite lunacy —
a sorcery dressed in rosepetals —
a fond interlocking   a twinning —
a small hum of joy in the heart

Have I lost the poems to love?
Unlikely   but even if so
it has been a healthy exchange —
a passing of pain   a tender completion —
I shall never regret it.